Innovation: Way of Experiencing Joy!

Monish Jirge (M.J.)
-An Innovation Enthusiast

The Joy Pledge

I am committed in dedicating this book to Richard Sheridan, who helped me in understanding the true essence of Joy and its implications towards innovation. Also, to all the fellow global leaders who think that "Joy is an important ingredient which directly affects Innovation".

The Joy Feeling

Every & any path for a human being is endless when it is filled with newer experiences. Every experience is a result of expectations, efforts and off course the way of execution. To enable all your current + new expectations, efforts and execution aspects one needs to be in a continuous state of fulfilled mind. One of the most prominent fulfilling elements is <JOY>.

What is Joy?

JOY = Jovial Outcome of Yield

JOY is an independent state of our soul which is helping us sail with full throttle in our path during our moments of excitement as well as endurance.

It is the only transferrable element which can only energize and excite a fellow human being or your fellow team mate.

The Joy Pillars

Joy mostly depends upon different aspects for each individual and organizations.

The pillars which I discovered are as follows:

Heads,

Hearts,

&

Hands

The JOY Pillars

JOY purely may depend upon our Heads, Hearts & our Hands.

The dependence is justified as follows:

Heads = What we think?

Hearts = How we feel?

Hands = Why we want to do it?

The Head Joy

What we think 24 hours is what we become is often said widely and wisely.

The way we think has a lot of impact on our own & the organizational progress.

Why The Head Joy Matters?

The topics of which when we think about and give us JOY are different, and can be lateral to each one's aspect of JOY.

The topics which can be influential and vital to our progress may or may not offer us JOY but are essential for our progress.

The Individual Head Joy

In order to continuously experience your own head joy, there needs to be a set of pendulum actions defined which are cyclical and balance out the joy emotions.

Define a daily & weekly joy schedule for yourself.

What is a Joy Schedule?

Before beginning with the joy schedule, asses your personal habits.

Write down your habits and ways to modify and change them for good.

Once you know define it, then start defining your topics which give or may provide you joy.

Schedule page

What is your Joy Schedule?

Habits:

1.

2.

3.

Joy topics:

1.

2.

3.

The Organizational Heads Joy

The pendulum balance will normally play a key role in balancing the joy of your team and their innovation capabilities.

Creating a joy landscape will boost the organizational heads joy.

What is joy landscape?

We have to analyze each and every topic of the team member which yields maximum output and joy for the individual and the organization as well.

Ask each team member of your organization about the topics which give him / her the maximum joy.

Analyze and segregate these topics from a functional perspective which means from an operations view point.

Collect the joy data of each employee and collate it, then form joy teams.

What are joy teams?

Joy teams are a group of people who enjoy thinking about similar topics.

Influencers of joy teams: Internal & External relationships

Internal relationships

Relationships which are within the company from different departments structures, job functions need to be on a common framework.

External relationships

Relationships which are outside the organization which may include customers, collaborators, etc.

Define your internal relationships

1.

2.

3.

Define your external relationships

1.

2.

3.

Innovating with the Head Joy

Now we have seen, about the joy elements of head joy.

Innovation comes at the intersection of diversity and not similarity.

Innovation will be at its peak when we combine the six hat thinking way with the joy teams where the people with similar joy statement will work together thinking about diverse ways with a focus on a solving a concrete problem.

The Heart Joy

Heart is an organ which heal and hinder a human being for its own and the overall organization progress.

Feeling is a subject which is often most probably and undecidedly ignored in most of our own lives and organizations.

It is a catalyst for Enjoyment.

En-joyment = Enabling-Joy

Feeling is the foundation of fair expressions resulting into foreseeable actions.

Feeling management

Managing your feelings or emotions can directly affect your productivity and efficiency

Efficiency = Effectively managing your feelings and actions

The feeling cluster

The feeling cluster is a simple way of creating a transparent structure where you and your team mates can transparently show about "how they are feeling today".

The feeling cluster will be feedback mechanism to reorganize their daily activity and delegate work according to their preferential feeling.

Innovation is bringing the feelings of everyone together and putting them into a feeling basket.

The Individual Heart Joy

Every person is unique and ubiquitous in having the control to his or her feeling.

The way to manage your feeling is to record it, find the ways to temporarily modify and cultivating the capability of changing it permanently.

The feelings depend upon instantaneous

way of our communication patterns.

Feeling record

Record your feelings along with the way you felt after communicating with those specific people.

2 questions arise:

With whom you communicated?

How you felt?

What can be improved to feel better?

Record both the above and cross-relate each of these.

Feeling record

With whom you talked?:

1.

2.

3.

What was the topic?:

1.

2.

3.

How you felt?:

1.

2.

3.

What can be improved to feel better?:

1.

2.

3.

The Organizational Heart Joy

An organization is a collective pot of feelings. The way people feel is directly related to the way they make other feel.

Feeling is a critical way of connecting internally and externally with your feel go factor.

Healing can help everyone from bottom to top to harvest best relationships for the best possibilities.

The Healing Way

Establishing healing as one of the verticals of your people management can do wonders who want their team mates not to wander and worry during their work.

Having weekly, monthly healing sessions can make it more relatable for the team to the company as well as themselves.

Having a healing group session can boost your feeling quotient.

The Healer Coaches

Since we have seen the vitality of feelings along with the way they influence

the performance.

Introducing a healing-mentoring program where personal and professional challenges are written down, analyzed, as well as co-related will clarify the picture for the employees and will give them a sense of

CARESHIP which is

"Caring Ownership"

Innovating with the Heart Joy

The feeling, healing and mentoring may lead us in discovering best possible communication patterns, team patterns and the way to lead with uncertainty.

This type of framework can be best utilized during crisis and the normal times.

Innovation will take place when the intentional and unintentional feelings are neutralized with this framework.

The Hand Joy

The creation of humanity has been possible with the symphony of our hands.

Anything which has been created has been only possible with our hands.

Hands and the confidence to carry out an activity can help us in creating History.

The Hand Joy

Ask each team member of your organization about the activities which give him / her the maximum joy.

Analyze and segregate these activities from a functional perspective which means from an operations view point.

Collect the joy data of each employee and collate it, then form teams.

What are historical teams?

Teams and people who want to create history with the creation they are aiming to achieve and built it.

The main way in building historical teams is to inspire and recognize their burning desire.

The historical questions

Define your historical teams?

Ask them what creation would make them

Feel historical?

Define rewards for creating history?

Innovating with Hands Joy

When there is a sense of creating history, people think beyond-the-box and go above & beyond limits in creating something which is valuable to their intentions.

Innovation can happen when such talent of historical team members come together.

Expectations, Efforts, Execution

According to my short journey in accompanying Innovation, the three most essential elements have been expectations, efforts and relentless execution.

Set expectations with empathy

Put efforts with endurance

Execute with energy!!

Truly Your,
A Joy Being,
Monish Jirge

www.ingramcontent.com/pod-product-compliance
Lightning Source LLC
Chambersburg PA
CBHW030045230526
45472CB00005B/1692